EXTRA INNINGS

New Poems by Raymond Souster

ISBN 0 88750 217 2 (hardcover)
ISBN 0 88750 218 0 (softcover)

Design: Michael Macklem. Cover: Rick/Simon.

Printed in Canada

PUBLISHED IN CANADA BY OBERON PRESS

Again for Rosalia

FEBRUARY MORNING, ELIZABETH STREET

I'm the only one out along Elizabeth Street
this twenty-one degree wind-snapping morning,
and I walk fast, coat collar up:
                                but no—
there's something there in the half-shadows
of this hotel doorway—a figure sitting huddled
in a corner where the ventilator exhaust above him
blows warm air reaching even to the street,
—and no again—it's a *her*, not a *him*,
an old wizened lady who sits back there
and reads from what looks like a pocket Bible, holding
the book up closely to her nose, and so intent on what she's
        reading
she doesn't see me go by—
                                and probably no-one else,
not even the world. I can only guess she has all
her earthly possessions in those two paper bags beside her,
but it seems the heat from the hotel and the book she's reading
are all she needs right now—she wouldn't thank me
for pity or money, probably wouldn't even be impressed
if the Prime Minister himself at this very moment
drove up in his limousine, and walking jauntily over,
offered her a sniff from the fresh pink carnation
glowing like all his promises in his buttonhole.

PICTURES FROM A LONG-LOST WORLD

Bloody Sunday, St. Petersburg, 22 January, 1905

Sunday morning, with an icy wind
driving flurries of snow through St. Petersburg,
George Gapon, priest, former prison chaplain,
leader of his "Assembly of Russian Workingmen"
(created and secretly directed by the police),
set out with his column marching from the Narva hall
while other clergy led other columns, all bent on assembling
outside the Winter Palace, where a petition
would be handed to the Czar.
                        The petition began:
"Sire, we working men and inhabitants of St. Petersburg,
our wives and our children, our helpless parents,
have come to you to seek truth, justice and protection. We
    have been made beggars;
we are oppressed and borne down by labour beyond our
    strength;
we are humiliated, we are not treated as human beings
but as slaves who must endure their bitter fate in silence,"
and ended: "And if you don't give these orders or respond to
    our pleas,
we shall die here in this square in front of your palace."

But the new Minister of the Interior,
Prince Mirsky, was ready. The soldiers—Guards,
Cossacks and Hussars, stopped Gapon's column
at the Narva arch.
                        When they refused to move away,
the horsemen galloped into them; when they reformed their
    ranks,
the troops opened fire. There were many wounded, many
    dying. . . .

And the Czar, who was not even in the city,
was moved to write in his diary: "A painful day:
there have been serious disorders in St. Petersburg
because workers wanted to come to the Winter Palace.
Troops had to open fire in several places of the city;
there were many killed and wounded. God, how painful and
    sad!
Mama arrived from town: straight to Mass.
I lunched with all the others.
Went for a walk with Misha.
Mama stayed overnight."

THE HOTTER IT GETS

"The hotter it gets, the cooler I get"
—President Richard Nixon, speech of 26 October, 1973

Not much of an advantage in heaven,
but what a trump card to have in hell!

TO A PORTRAIT PAINTER

You are content
to paint masks.

I must wait
for those masks
to slip down.

8

JANUARY WOODS

Nothing stirring in these woods but me
and one helter-skelter squirrel.

From this downhill stream not a gurgle;
a last sound froze in its throat
perhaps about an hour past midnight.

Now view the treasure of the hour:
between the wizened wild-hop pods
branches on which hang clusters
of blood-red berries—
                              and instantly reborn
the wild lipstick smear of your lips
inching toward me—melting, plunging me back
into the summer of a memory. . . .

THE FORD HOTEL COMING DOWN

The Ford Hotel coming down
this month of February, 1974,
floor by cautious floor.
                              Today
they must be down to the fifteenth
which would make it three below the floor
where ten years ago I hired out Charles Olson
a room for two nights.
                              I say a room,
but when I called on him that first day at noon,
saw his six-foot-six, two hundred eighty pounds crowded into
     it,
"band-box" would have been more fitting. . . .

But those were meagre times; Charles Olson was a name
to only a few, and we'd brought him up to read
at Av Isaac's Greenwich Gallery on a shoestring,
so every dollar spent on his hotel meant that much less
for booze and food, in that order.
                              And I can still see the size
of that steak he ate in Steele's, remember him downing
half a bottle of Cutty Sark during intermission
the night of his reading.
                              But everything he did was huge, grand
     or overpowering,
from the long booming lines of his verse to his five-planed
     conversations,
his whisky intake—

though the night we sat in the Towne,
drank beer, dug Ray Bryant's very blue piano
over the bar's chatter-clatter, I drank as much as he did,
and pushed out with him at closing-time onto yellow-glowing,
    snow-covered Yonge Street
almost sober, to shake hands solemnly, watch him amble easily
    off
up toward the Strip, everyone who passed him by
doing a big double-take, and no doubt wondering
what a professional wrestler was doing out at midnight in
    Toronto,
his toque pulled well down, shuffling away through the snow.

THE ELEPHANT IN THE MANCHADI SEED

These pea-like seeds grow on the Manchadi tree, the redwood of India. The top of each seed is cut off and the seed is hollowed out. The craftsman then carves a tiny elephant from a waste chip of ivory, which his more fortunate brothers have discarded from their work and sold to him. He puts the tiny elephant in the seed, carving an ivory plug for the top. It is said, in India, that the buyer of a Manchadi seed receives ten times God's good luck, but if he should buy the seed and give it away, he will receive a hundred times God's good luck. These seeds come from Kerala in Southern India.....

I

Although I've told him
there isn't room for two,
my elephant's so lonely
that he's finally got desperate,
put an ad in the papers,

and is waiting for Monday,
when he hopes the mail brings him
five or six replies.

2

He seems to grow smaller
every time I look at him,
so I wouldn't be too surprised
if some day when I look in

there's not even a grain
of white ivory left
to show he ever was.

FIRST SKATER

Leaving behind
at every turning
scratched circles
of delicious joy.

PICTURES OF A LONG-LOST WORLD

Hong Kong, 1941

"You bastards are going with me
right to the top and we'll kill
every one of those bloody Japs,"
Sergeant-Major John Robert Osborn
told his sixty-five men,

(all that was left of B Company,
Winnipeg Grenadiers, a regiment
"not recommended for operational training,"
on December 19, 1941):

and a half-hour later
with thirty men left
he stormed to the top
of Mount Butler, then stayed there
for eight hours and a half.

(Able seaman at Jutland,
a farmer in Saskatchewan,
Manitoba railway worker,
now at forty-two
a soldier at Hong Kong)

"Dig, you sons-of-bitches,
dig like you've never dug before,
they'll be back for us soon,"
he told them with a grin.

(Mr. Ralston,
Canadian Minister of Defence:
"The garrison's position is undoubtedly,
for the time being, a very trying
and difficult one":
John Osborn,
his bayonet thick with blood,
an ugly gash on his forearm,
would have damn well agreed with him. . . .)

And the Japs came back,
slinging grenades by the dozen,
and soon there were twelve,
then only six Grenadiers;
finally five as Osborn
threw himself on a grenade
he couldn't reach in time. . . .

Is there still a Mount Butler
in Hong Kong today?
If there is it should be called
John Osborn's Hill.

JUST TO WATCH YOU SMOKING

Just to watch you smoking
sets me on edge tonight.

Inhale
and I slip down your throat,

exhale
and I curl from your nostrils,

all the time glowing fire-red
between your fingertips.

BEGGAR

Only a cupped hand
to hold out.

POLITICIANS

They all make
great poker players.

For them the game
is everything.
No stakes too high.
And if they lose

they shrug their shoulders,
wait for the next deal,
(there always seems to be another)

then push their chips out
recklessly as ever.

You, I,
feel their sweaty fingers
as we form the pot

they recklessly build
in the centre of our world.

THE NEW NEGLIGEE

Diaphonous green
shading white
sheltering black!

THE DUKE'S LAST ONE-NIGHT STAND

He must have logged a million miles
on planes trains buses
especially buses.

His music his life,
that band his single instrument.

Then one night he had a gig
in a town he'd never heard of before.
Disasterville, he dubbed it right away
when nobody had showed at the terminal,
when they found the ballroom in darkness.
It was all some big mistake,
but no matter,
he was too tired to straighten it out
and went to bed early.

In the morning
he woke to find himself all alone,
with no plans made to take him anywhere.
Then I'll go back to bed,
sleep in a little, he decided.

It was cool in the room.
It was nice to be going nowhere for a change.
He didn't care if they ever wakened him.

PICTURES FROM A LONG-LOST WORLD

Eamon de Valera after capture at Boland's Mill,
30 April, 1916

"Shoot me if you want to
but take care of my men," de Valera says grim-faced
to the young English officer who's just arrived
to take the surrender. A surrender he's fought against
since the night before, when Pearse and the Volunteers
had turned in their arms.
                              Now hatless, unkempt,
his long legs wrapped in untidy leggings,
his once proud grey-green uniform
soiled with flour dust and dirt,
he's marched away, brown eyes staring straight ahead,
while the street crowd looks on in silence.

But the Commandant doesn't see their faces: in his tiredness
all the week spins through his head—

White clouds of Easter Sunday morning,
first shots at noon sounding in the distance
as his Third Battalion covers Boland's Mill
and Westland Row Station, where Pearse has told him
the English troops will advance from. Battalion headquarters
    set up
in Boland's Bakery. Tuesday, grey and dark with rain, little
    action.

Wednesday clear and warm, and a gunboat from the River
finally lobs a shell close by. Then English troops advance
toward Mount Street Bridge, but his snipers pick them off
with ease: he himself can't sleep, roams the positions
urging on his men, some of them little more than boys.
Then Thursday, with Dublin in flames and the British closing
     in,
he knows the end's not far off. Friday he learns O'Connell
     Street's in ruins,
flames eating at the Post Office, Connolly badly wounded
carried out on a stretcher. Then Black Saturday, when Pearse
     and his men
stack their arms at the Parnell Monument—he hadn't believed
     the news at first,
thinking it a trick; then the courier from Pearse
finally convinces him it's true.
                                        Now what's ahead?
Prison? A firing squad? What will happen
to Sinead, the four young ones?
It's all in the hands of God, he knows, the tears welling,
they and Ireland as well.
                              "Ah, but if the people
had only come out with knives and forks even...."

MY MEMORY OF THE MEMRAMCOOK VALLEY

The best farming land
in all New Brunswick,
with certainly
the most cunning farmers,

nine of whom—
eight Cormiers
and one Gaudet—
(that Gaudet on the team
because either his brother
was the neighbourhood priest
or because he had
the best pitching arm,
I forget which),
battled us on the diamond
one sunny Wednesday afternoon:

and me, the big-city hurler,
my curve breaking sharp in warm-up,
expected the game to be a breeze,
but found out the very first inning
there's just no way you can win
against an umpire not calling corners
who doesn't speak or won't understand English,
even when you let him know he stinks. . . .

We lost that game 4–2
and cursed all the way back to camp
that we'd ever set foot in that valley,
the valley of the Memramcook.

YOUR FELLOW AMERICANS

Best people
best country

the freest
most brave

never able
to spread it
very thin.

BURNING

Spring
kindles and re-
kindles: burns me
in its kind-
ling.

THAT DAY OF THE SMALL WINDS

That day of the small winds
I swear, when you got right under
and in among trees, you heard
the clear click click of leaves
breaking from lifetime branches
one at a time, sailing out
and down and down.

But the next day
was one of big winds only,
wave-smash, wave-moan,
the only noise the shriek
of winds pounding onshore, reeling,
flung back upon themselves.

No separate click
of any leaf: any ones that voyaged that day
did so unceremoniously, caught up
in the anonymous death
of thousands plucked and whirled
in a vortex of terror.

So no-one quite believed
that day of the small winds ever was.

SHORT CONVERSATION

"Where do you have your shoes fixed?"

"At a place down the street;
I've known the shoemaker since a boy,
he's Polish, same as you."

"He's not Polish, he's Jewish."

"If he comes from Poland
that makes him Polish, doesn't it?"

"It still only makes him a Jew."

AND NOW PAUL BLACKBURN

Up here even bad news
travels slow.
                    So it was only today
that I read of your death
on September 13, 1971
in Mr. Ellmann's new anthology.
That would make it
twelve years ago, give or take a month,
that we braved New York's pitiless heat, its clang-clashing
     traffic
to search out your office—Funk and Wagnall's, no less—
where you finally emerged, very small, very youthful looking,
and smiling, apologetic for having kept us waiting:
"So damn hard for me to tear myself away
from my work, folks,"
                    then plunging out
into the waiting blast furnace
of lower Manhattan, where we let you lead us
through block after block of dirty streets, rotting houses,
until we stopped at a restaurant, which you said
had the best Puerto Rican food in town, and where inside
your three friends joined us at the biggest table,
and we talked about nothing really for over an hour,
with the only thing I remember the cold beer from San Juan
     and taking one look
at my seafood plate and not being able
to do more than pick at it while everybody else
ate with the greatest gusto.

Then we said goodbye
on the street outside and you were gone, with me not knowing
any more now than I had before about you.

All of which isn't much to hang a poem on,
so let me say simply: at your best
you were one of the sharpest, most honest
of your generation, and the only poet
with a love-affair going for your crazy-mad city
that never once cooled.
                    Or as a friend of yours wrote me:
"Even to our last connection—the day before
he was told he was dying of cancer."

UNEXPECTEDLY

Unexpectedly, from
tall meadow grass
beside the booming river,

a crow, cawless,
unflapped a sooted spread
of wings, flew up,
ghost risen
against the crisp morning;

leaving this image:
Death rising unheralded,
evil bird
smudging the beloved light.

THE CABLEGRAM

Over the telephone
the cablegram saying it
so swiftly
so finally

PAPPA MORTO
PIETRO

While they wonder how
and where
and why

And here it is again
printed out
on this piece of paper

so easy
not so easy
to understand

PAPPA MORTO
PIETRO

THE MOON

cooly
there

WATCHING AIRCRAFT TAKE OFF FOR GERMANY

For Carl Schaefer

Tonight they're the lucky ones
who watch from the tarmac
their comrades lifting up,
who'll later turn in sleep
hearing the engine-roar
of those even luckier ones
who've managed to come home.

And tomorrow night the ones
who've come home will watch these,
the watchers of tonight,
as they lift off, outbound.

And night after night
all that will ever change
will be the aircraft,
the faces watching them,

the war certainly will not change,
will have the same lusty appetite
for flesh.

THE BOOKS IN MY BOOKCASE

The books in my bookcase
though their covers stay clean,
brightly-coloured as ever,

have their pages yellowing
some badly, some faintly,
smell no longer fresh.

We are growing old—
imperceptibly,
uncomplainingly—
together.

THE BLACK AND THE GREY

The black squirrel
after the grey squirrel
and now
the grey one
after the black.

My little cat
doesn't really care
who chases who,
not as long
as they still twist and dart
faster than even
her eye can follow,
her tail twitch after.

COUNTY COURT ROOM 21

Did the tough-faced
long-haired kid standing up in court
and telling the judge
I don't need no lawyer,
trace with his finger on this dust-covered
window of the courtroom john
I HATE FUCKIN COPS?

I doubt it; he's under arrest
and couldn't come here alone:
("He received three years for robbery
on Friday, Your Honour,
today it's two charges
of assault causing bodily harm.")

But somebody wrote it this morning,
and I say to the policeman
washing his hands beside me,
"You've got another fan letter there,"
and he looks at me and smiles,
for he has a perfect right to smile,
he lives with this every day,
eats with it, sleeps with it,
a monotonous diet
with few laughs in between.

But not one of us "honest"
"upright" citizens
has any right to smile,
or be smug,
or to think it's the least bit funny:

come down to Court Room 21,
Old City Hall, Toronto,
any day Monday to Friday,
10 AM to 4 PM,
sit on one of these overcrowded benches,
look at the kids poorly clothed,
swaggering tough with their sixteen-year-old girlfriends,
waiting for their cases to come up,
talking so glibly about remands,
convictions, suspended sentences,
the way the rest of us talk about the weather
or the score of the latest hockey game.

Each kid with a lawyer
to go into court with,
but no parents anywhere,
the Salvation Army
the only ones here
who give a good goddamn.

Yet I can walk away
from all this misery,
take my wife
to a fashionable place for lunch,
eat the kind of a meal
not one in a hundred
of these kids ever sees,

and still not lean over
our balcony looking down
on the diners below
in their smart smart clothes
and throw it all up,

either because I don't believe
this evil can be changed,
this system I've helped create,
help perpetuate,
(and so I don't let it
really get to me),

or maybe I don't mind too much
the way it works,
the way it destroys,

and because I may hope
to buy off my conscience
by writing a page or two
of angry verse.

SUN

Blind with your radiance
my blindness
O all-renewing fire!

OLD WOMAN ON YONGE STREET

Just by the way
this old Chinese woman
inches her way up the street,
one hand clutching her bag
the other one leaning all her weight
on store-fronts, the sides of buildings,

you feel there's no way she'll make it
for another single block,

but probably some sad-sack like me
had the very same agonizing thought
a block or so farther down from here.

THE WEEK OF THE SMALL LEAVES

The week of the small leaves is over,
those small, softly-green spring banners
hung down on every street.

From now on every tree will groan
under the weight of its branches,
its thick-matted harvest of summer,
each leaf thick-veined, stretching out full fingers.

The week of the small leaves is over,
that first delicate wonder disappearing
under a riot of abundance.

PICTURES FROM A LONG-LOST WORLD

Dien Bien Phu, 1954

You can almost see Colonel Piroth,
artillery commander, making the appropriate gestures
as he recites over and over
to every visitor: "Firstly, the Viet-Minh
won't have a chance of getting their guns
through to here; secondly, if they do
we'll smash them, and even if they manage
to somehow keep on shooting they won't be able
to get enough ammo to do any harm."

Or Colonel de Castries, on being asked
if the strong points around the airstrip
permit its effective defence, tells General Bodet
there are no worries on that score. And when other visitors
complain about strongpoint Gabrielle,
the closeness of ammunition dumps
to the parking areas of the aircraft,
and even that by April fifteenth the fortress
will be a marsh drowning in the monsoon rains,

there are reassuring answers ready,
and always the honour guard receptions
at the airfield by Moroccans in gleaming white turbans,
Legionaires at strongpoint Beatrice, lunch with gleaming table
    service
at the command mess, or perhaps a reconnaissance
in a new tank with the paratroopers
to reassure the most dubious. . . .

While all this time the enemy
is opening a road through the jungle,
a jungle road of five hundred miles
with twenty thousand coolies sweating three long months
to widen roads to take 105 mm. howitzers,
120 mm. mortars, recoilless rifles,
and 800 Russian trucks—
"Everything for the Front,
Everything for Victory" . . . .

So now we have arrived at March 13, 1954.
A few rain squalls
have fallen on this small, very green
North Vietnamese valley,
but otherwise it is quiet
with the rising smoke of the many cooking fires,
with the laundry laid out to dry
over the strands of barbed wire. . .

But tonight at 1700 hours
the first Viet-Minh bombardment
will bury bunker after bunker, trench after trench,
on strongpoint Beatrice.
                    And hell will be reborn
to flame unchecked till one rainy day in May. . . .

DIETRICH BONHOEFFER AT THE GALLOWS

The noose
fitting snugly like a parson's collar.

PILE-DRIVER

If this pile-driver
keeps driving
it's going to drive me
to the same place it's driven
all other piles.

FEDERAL ELECTION, ANY YEAR

At this moment in time,
one week before election day,
we are pleased to present you
with the following statistics:

Liberals: 42
Conservatives: 34
NDP: 18

Of course let us hasten to add
that figures sometimes fail
to tell the whole story,
or to truly reflect the mood of the electors,

so although these figures
representing as they do
the number of wilfully-destroyed election signs
as counted by our survey in the riding,
can be taken as correct,

they still don't take into account
those other signs carefully shredded, dropped down corner
    sewers,
or those carefully piled and hidden in the parks,

and therefore do not totally reflect
the childishness, the petty spitefulness
so hard at work in this campaign.

LITTLE BAT AT LAST BROKEN

For George Bowering

Yankee-made in the Adirondacks
of solid mountain ash,
black-coloured, wavy grain, light to swing,
this bat took me through twenty seasons
of softball good and bad, and while I stuck with her
gave me few strike-outs, many base hits,
(not big hits, mind you, but the kind
most ball games are won by).
                              And so today
like a fool I took this last souvenir
of so many sweat-filled, nerve-tingling innings,
along to the office game, maybe thinking what the hell
it's probably the last time you'll ever play,
so why not go down swinging with Little Bat in your hands?

Which probably would have been all right
only I wasn't content, had to shoot my big mouth off
about how great my bat was, even calling it the Ron Hunt
    Special,
which was a lot of bs
                        But anyway, some jerk
finally took it to the plate with him, didn't hold the label up,
and on the first pitch broke it clean in half,
with everybody on the field laughing hard but me,

and I was so mad with myself
I didn't even take it home
after the game, left it lying there in the park,
still handsome somehow, still the greatest Little Bat,
but broken now in two, not to be used again,
a piece of dead wood
I couldn't stand to look at any more.

THE DAY FRANCO DIED

He died, finally, today,
El Caudillo, Spain's great one,
and though you could say it was unkind,
I couldn't help giving out
with one great inward cheer,

because my good Catholic friend
had told me if Franco lived
until Saturday he'd win the prayers
of the Holy Mother herself,
be whisked straight off to heaven;

this way, by dying on Thursday,
he may be forced
to take a thousand-year detour
through the seven kingdoms of hell.

ALREADY

Already we've watched float away
our last gulped-down
one-minute-to-ten pint
of mild and bitter.

Already we've roamed the streets
noisy with election sound-trucks,
looking for something
we're not very liable to find.

Already met
the two Land Army girls
as the Fun Fair closed,
the ones who gave us each
a pull from the bottles of beer
they carried in the pockets
of their loose-fitting coats.

Already we've felt the chill
of night coming on,
already watched the darkness
shutting us slowly off
from a living world.

Already known the full curse
of being in uniform,
of being far from home
of being very young.

Already we've lived a lifetime
with midnight still half an hour away.

THESE WILD CRAB-APPLES

No bigger than cherries,
skin-shrivelled, pulp-empty,

these wild crab-apples
nevertheless cling hard
to their wind-tortured branches,

though being dead
they need not fear death.

But looking at them
from my safe window,
this must be the thing
that frightens me.

THE SAILOR AND THE AIRMAN

First time I ever saw a forty-ouncer
was in the hands of a boyish-looking sailor
in the walkway between two coaches
of the Montreal–Toronto pool train.

He offered me a slug right away,
and after I'd grabbed the bottle carefully,
tipped it back, the Hudson Bay rum first burned
my throat, then my stomach all the way
to my toes and back, then down again.

That was just out of Montreal;
I didn't see him again until near Toronto
when I crossed between coaches again
on my way to the washroom—there he was,
bottle three-quarters empty, beautiful smile
of no pain at all across his face
as he waved the hand holding the bottle—
while I wondered how he still stood up.

But I knew sailors do a lot of drinking
and usually manage quite well: and besides
the train was now at Broadview Station,
with the next stop Union—I was home again!

But I'd hardly stepped off that train,
joined the crowd hurrying to the exits
when I saw my sailor again. Somehow he'd managed
to step off the coach, but was now half-leaning,
half-falling down against a signal-post,
still that stupid grin on his face,
but no bottle now in his hand
(only a tightly packed duffel bag)
and a look of bewilderment in his eyes
because his legs just wouldn't work any more.

What the hell, I said under my breath,
stopped beside him, grabbed him by the arm,
asked him where he was heading for.
                                    Hamilton,
I was sure he answered, so I started half-walking,
half-carrying him along the station platform,
then up the endless stairs to the upper level
where the Hamilton-Buffalo train would be waiting,
and made it, but only, to the first coach of the train,
and had my sailor half-pushed up the steps
when the conductor came running down the platform,
tapped me on the shoulder, yelled in my ear
that I wasn't putting any drunk on his train
to puke in all the aisles.

So I hauled my sailor down,
held him up while I argued with the bastard,
giving him every cliché in the book
about fighting for King and Country,
how this poor sailor boy from Halifax
couldn't afford to miss a day of his leave,
with a crowd collecting as we stood there,
(but not one of those dummies said a word,
they were just there for the show).
                              Finally I saw
I was fighting a losing game, grabbed my sailor
more tightly by the arm, walked him back down the platform.
We'd only gone three or four coach lengths
when the train whistle sounded, and saying
to myself it's now or never,
and with the last strength in my arms,
I pushed, half-hoisted my sailor
up the nearest train-step, sat him down on the walkway,
then jumped off with the train moving under me.

And that was how a three-day leave
began for me August, 1944:
                              and that sailor?
I guess I'll never know now for sure if he got off
at Hamilton or Buffalo. . . .

FOR EUSTACE, GONE

In Memoriam, W.W.E. Ross, 1894–1966

Warmed by fine rye
I stood on your porch
that summer night, listening
to your voice grown eloquent
telling of talk with the dead,
experiments with spirits
all done with a scientist's
strict honest love
of truth.
          So, if by any chance
you're listening tonight,
Eustace, I still read
your plain good words,
think well of you.

Rommel at the gates of Egypt, Tobruk, June 1942

He remembers now his first staff meeting
in Tripoli, his fists clenched to emphasize his words:
"We must save Tripolitania
from the attack of the British Army.
We *will* hold them."
                        That was March '41,
the same month the British High Command had announced
in an intelligence summary: "Detachments of a German
    Expeditionary Force
under an obscure general, Rommel,
have landed in North Africa."
                        Those were lean times,
the months of see-saw battle. First he'd driven Neame
back behind Benghasi, then Derna, but Tobruk
was a nut he couldn't crack, though he'd used his men,
his armour as relentless nut-cracker.
                        Then in June
he'd bloodied Wavell's nose as Operation Battleaxe
died before his Panzer IV's with the new 50 mm.
Then it was eat sand and flies until November
when a new British general, Cunningham, had attacked him
only five days before his own carefully worked-out offensive
was due to take Tobruk once and for all.

                                          At the start
he'd had the Tommies on the run, and but for the stubbornness
of Auchinleck would have seized Tobruk, a prize it seemed
always just out of reach. Then it was he
in the end who'd had to withdraw, losing Badia
and then the Halfaya Pass. Followed by four months of
    idleness
used to build up his strength before he'd attacked again,
first blunting his sword
against the gallant French at Bir Hakim, then breaking out
at Gazala to smash the Eighth Army under Ritchie. . . .

And now, with dawn breaking, June 20, 1942,
he stands at his El Adem headquarters
watching Stukas dive-bomb Tobruk, and knows
that city's days are numbered, the road to Egypt
at last open. Even with oil short, tanks battered, men
    exhausted,
he feels nothing can stop him now. He'll press on
to Mersa Matruh, then follow to El Alamein—
and after that, Cairo!
                            Cairo, his brain
turns the word over slowly, savouring its sweetness. . .
Egypt, Suez, then Persia, Turkey!
His eyes crinkle at their edges
as he half-smiles to himself, which is all
a Field Marshal can allow at any time. . .
Why, if my Tigers roll again, who knows
we may never stop again till we've conquered the world!

FOR ROBERT FULFORD

What we had then
was innocence, Bob,

a word we killed
for your generation
and the next and the next

with our Belsens
our Dresdens
our Hiroshimas.

Don't forgive us, Bob,
only try a little harder
to understand us.

MY WORLD

My world
like the sun
must reach everywhere.

A VISITOR TO OUR LUNCH ROOM

Did he see our sign
posted so conspicuously
as you enter the door?

Or maybe he doesn't give a damn
for signs any more,
especially those saying
KEEP OUT
NO HELP WANTED
ENTER AT YOUR OWN RISK
(what has he really got to lose?)

Or maybe he's had
a few too many,
never saw any sign at all,
any more than he'd pay attention
to a red light at a corner crossing.

Anyway, I'm no sooner up from my chair
and half-way across the room,
when he comes in quickly, crosses to my table,
and sits down like it's the natural thing to do
in a crowded room with everybody busy eating
chicken casserole or roast-beef sandwiches.

Only he looks uncomfortable
only he must know he doesn't belong here,
not because anyone says a single word
(they don't, they all simply hide
behind their casseroles, their roast-beef sandwiches),

and he sits there drumming his fingers on the table,
facing the door, not looking at anyone,
a beaten man maybe in his sixties,
face lined with seams of age and dirt,
clothes unpressed and hanging ashamed to his body,
glad I suppose to get in out of the bitter cold
blowing torture up there on the street,
glad to see human faces relaxed
not one with a look of hate at him

which he gets every minute
of every hour
of every rotten day.

I don't wait any longer,
I know how this will end,
and there's nothing I can do
really nothing anyone can do.

I go out the door
leaving him sitting there
like a strange fish out of water
not knowing what to do any more.

Later at the office I hear it:
some bum right off the street
came in and sat at a table
and they finally had to ask him to leave.

So I only hope they asked him politely,
and it would have been nice if someone
had offered him hot coffee and a sandwich,

but that would have been too much
like praying for a miracle.

52

COUNTING

My big cat Max
allows me to sit beside him
on the grass.

Above us
from the overladen branches
of our wild crab-apple tree,
the apples fall one by one
with a small thud in the grass.

He counts the odd numbers
I count the even.

Between us
with any luck
we should easily reach three hundred
before bedtime.

PICTURES OF A LONG-LOST WORLD

Last Bunker Days, Führerbunker, Reich Chancellery, Berlin,
25–28 April, 1945

"Only a few months ago I'd have sworn the Führer
was turning yellow, no doubt from all those potions
Herr Doktor Morell mixes in his witch's brew...
now he's turned grey-white, much like the dust
coming in choking clouds down the ventilators
after those cursed Russian shellings,
and when last night he learned of Himmler's negotiations
he grew whiter still, almost white as the spittle
forming on his lips as he cursed *der treue Heinrich*
and Goering in the same breath—what was left
now his two most trusted friends had betrayed him?"

"A very good question: for the General Staff report
this morning shows the Russians a scant thousand metres
from our bunker. True, the Wannsee bridges still stand
waiting Wenck's arrival, but how long can two thousand
    Jugend
hold off Red Army tanks? And what good further tactics
using armies that have no ammunition
even if they had enough soldiers?
                              No wonder late last night
in the middle of that terrible bombardment,
Hitler announced his plan to die with Eva
and made us pledge to die with him. Who could not
be stirred enough to promise anything
in such a fiery presence?

Now the word tonight
is that within the next few hours he'll marry
his beloved Eva, then they'll drink champagne
with a few friends, no doubt toasting happier times,
and after that, who knows? No doubt he'll have
a last will and testament to leave
to a Germany that's failed him—his legacy
to future generations—and finally perhaps
he'll name a successor. After that,
what's left but to wait the right time
to die a soldier's death by his own hand,
with Eva to accompany him?"

"And come to think of it,
what's left for any of us who suffocate
in this living, clammy tomb,
doomed prisoners of our faith,
our fanatical devotion?
                          Poison, a bullet,
Russian firing-squad or prison?
Unless we shake ourselves loose of all this fear,
climb up the bunker steps and die as soldiers,
as Germans dying for the Fatherland."

"And now I'll end this last letter
I'll never have the chance to send."

THE HEROES

Not Wolfe or Montcalm
not Mackenzie, Papineau,

not even Riel
loveliest loser of all!

But Hull of the lightning shot,
old ageless Number Nine
with the shiftiest moves of all,
O bull-charging Rocket,
phantom Pocket,
the Big M with his eagle's glide—

these are our heroes,
born of hockey wars,

we who never quite grew up,
who carry our first sticks with us,
still shooting pucks
from cradle to the grave!

THAT FIRST DEATH

Some can even pinpoint
the hour of the day,
day of the week,
when they suddenly realized
they were dead.

For others
it's a more gradual process,
sneaking up on them
almost unnoticed,
such a little at a time.

A lot more people
are never aware of it,
truly,
the whole length of their lives.

But know it or not
it happens to all of us
at some point along the way.

And here is the problem:
the lungs keep breathing
the heart keeps pumping,
we have to go on living
have to go through the motions. . . .

Don't ask me why

dead men never have any answers.

THE BRIEF BUT ACHING SEASON

Now begins the brief but aching season
all leaves hate short of loathing; when they find themselves
    numbed,
clinging to branches with fingernails
ripped and close to bleeding,
and even then nothing certain

except that at some moment of some hour
a blast of wind will strike from east, from west,
and hiss at every branch, "let go, let go,"

and down one leaf will sail and then another,
swept on to death, father, mother, sister, brother.

PICTURES OF A LONG-LOST WORLD

Passchendaele, October 1917

Half-drowning in the miserable lean-to
that was really just a roof over mud,
my father heard a strange *plop plop plop*
almost on top of him, panicked, yelled at Fred
who was drowsing beside him, and with both hands shaking,
somehow pulled his gas-mask on.
                              But old Fred
wasn't buying it this time, he was sick of false alarms,
so didn't move until the first yellow cloud
seeped in a minute later (my father watching
through his half-fogged goggles, heard Fred cough,
then struggle with his gas-mask, cough, clutch his throat again,
then jump up, scramble out, a madman screaming
as he ran for the battery gas-curtain. . . .)

Six months later he was back
his lungs almost good as new.

THE STAG

"Eat it, eat it"
they cried,
beer voices shearing
the tobacco haze.

On his knees,
cold sober now,
mouth moving
toward that hairy thing,

he realized,
suddenly relaxed,
that this was not
the final degradation—

the day after tomorrow
he was taking as his own
another one like this.

THE LAST OF THE ROSES

I have brought you the last of the roses
but it's very plain to see
that my thought was wasted—yes, resented—
then it came to me suddenly why:

even in their petal-drooped,
shrivelled-stemmed slow dying,
they're so brazenly, mockingly alive
placed beside your living death!

THE VERY LAST GAME

If you're feeling very charitable
you can even forgive him
this last baseball lie:

(somehow managing
to stay on his feet
through all nine innings,
and in the fourth
breaking the tie-game wide open
with a deep shot to centre
that the fielder misjudged),

which our still-eager rookie
of fifty-three years
stretched out after game-time
to a grand-slam drive,

although there were runners
at only second and third
when his big fluke came. . . .

THE RELUCTANT FEET

Since her earliest rememberings
she had the surest feeling
her right foot wanted
to go one way,
her left foot the other.

No use to tell her mother,
she'd only laugh at her,
so she endured all those years
with one foot tugging south
the other north,
and no matter how hard she pleaded
with that unruly pair
they wouldn't listen at all.

Then when she was married
she carried her secret
like a small nagging cancer
eating slowly at her heart. . . .

Now see her today
middle-aged, all alone,
walking up Lansdowne Avenue
in boots reaching up to her ankles,
with the right toe pointing north
with the left toe pointing south,

and though she knows people laugh,
shake their heads behind her back,
she's happy to have two feet
that can go the way they want to go,

and who knows?—perhaps in time
they'll tire of walking opposite directions,
even end up shuffling together?

But she's grown rather old for miracles
and her feet are very set in their ways,
so she'd be the most surprised of all
if this suddenly should happen to her.

Now much more likely she thinks
they'll simply change with each other—
and the right toe will then point south
and the left toe point due north,

and she wonders if the day that happens
she'll be able to laugh at all
at those two feet who rule her life.

THE RESPONSE

The tree's branches
knocked against our window:
It wanted to be friends
and come in.

My answer was to open my window
reach out and hack off
its two longest arms.

A SUNNY DAY FOR THE WEDDING

At least they'll start off
all light and air and sunshine.

OLD SOLDIERS

Old soldiers never die—
they live on to send their sons off
to other wars.

FATAL ACCIDENT

This is how
we want to remember her—

long golden hair
back-dropped against
a black dress covering
full-shaped, active body,
and under the face-curls
eyes darting out
from behind their glasses
with a mocking tenderness
that made you her prisoner—

not the face ripped to ribbons
transfixed in the windshield,
not the chest
where the steering-wheel punched through,
not that blond head splattered with blood
much too red to be real. . . .

(Some of us ask
why, why?—
to sharpen the pain)

COST

It's nice to give
for a change
(he writes me)
when it doesn't cost anything.

As if you can ever
put a price

on caring
on love.

THE NEXT TIME

The next time someone tells me
the world is going mad

I'll have to answer, no,
that's not quite accurate:

it's already gone.

WATERFOWL

To come on you dead
in a morning shouting out
live! live! live!
in bird-song, sun-shafting,
cloud-billow, river-roar. . .

Dead in the long grass
not ten feet from running water,
red gash on your breast
slashing at my unprepared heart.

So that both hands shook
as I picked you up, carried you
by the webbed feet to sullen river bank,
then slung you out, watched your body
fall brown and limp into seething water,

to sink, then bob up, begin the short
burial journey to the lake, your blue
and untroubled final home.

RAIN

Rain
tear-dripping
at my window

take your sadness
somewhere else

we're full up here.

61 SQUADRON

The wonderful matter-of-factness
of the unsung hero:

"Somehow we got ahead of the stream
on the Turin show,
so had to circle Mont Blanc
almost half an hour, for the moment
killing nothing but time."

THE ANSWER

Why, my wife asked me
the other night,
do the bellies of starving children
swell up to bursting,
I'd have thought they'd go the other way.

And for once I didn't have an answer,
any answer.
        Then last night
in my dream a thousand balloons
danced and frolicked in the sky,
until Death rode by in his space-machine
and laughingly pricked each one
with his very sensitive needle. . . .

Ah, I remember thinking in my dream,
there's the answer,
now my only problem is to remember
to tell it to my wife in the morning.

IN THE PADDY WAGON

He's very drunk
he's screaming as he kicks
and swearing as he kicks
the door of the paddy wagon,

but there's no way he'll break it down
it's only him who'll be broken,
his strength if not his spirit.

In the meantime the two policemen
in the front seat of the van
have a smile every time he kicks
and another every time he swears,

and the people on the street smile too
and several give a nervous laugh,
but I know that I can't smile
and certainly can't laugh,

because there's a man in there,
there's a human being locked up tight
in that narrow, sweaty metal box,

and but for the grace of God
it could be either you or me,
trapped like some animal
sick in the mind with only
the instinct to go free
still burning on in our brain,

with only four walls to kick
that keep laughing, smiling back.

PICTURES FROM A LONG-LOST WORLD

Colonel-General Franz Conrad von Hötzendorf arrives at
the Lemberg Station after the victorious Gorlice-Tarnow
Offensive, June 1915

As he poses with his staff on the station platform
there's no smile on the seamed old face, the eyes aren't
    sparkling as usual. And this at a time
when a victory has finally come—the Carpathians cleared,
Russian troops running in their thousands. But although it's
    his battle-plan,
Mackensen is really in command, the Eleventh Army of the
    Germans
has really made the break-through: while his quick war with
    Serbia
has ground to a halt, his armies driven back across the Danube
with over 200,000 in losses—all this from a third-rate nation
he'd planned would collapse in three weeks!
                                Now the Empire
is the laughing-stock of the Continent, his best officers
and NCOs slaughtered, his armies weary
of chasing or being chased by the Russian hordes.

So though he can't smile today, he hasn't given up:
Ludendorff and his colonel have a brilliant scheme
that could knock Russia out of the war,
end the nightmare stalemate on two fronts,
and mean final victory in another year,
victory for Austria and his Emperor!
The Old Corpse of Europe still very much alive!

But there's a catch, of course, like everything else—
first the plan must go to Posen
and the Kaiser's Conference—and Falkenhayn it's well known
has his eyes still fixed on France, the *Ost*
is still a sideline to him.
                            Still, as the Colonel-General leaves
        the station
his mood lifts, he steps almost lightly
into his staff car. Surely things must go right
from now on, this war I wanted soon over.

So that he can manage a smile
as *that* voice answers him right back:
Von Hötzendorf, not *this* war!

OLD MAN IN THE CONCOURSE

One thing you can count on
he doesn't come here to read world news in the *Sun*,
or to eat the garbage these restaurants disguise as food,
or to sit in the bar of the tavern, have his mind blown cleanly
    by the noise of amplified rock,
or to stare at the jiggle of passing posteriors, the bounce of
    brassièreless breasts,
or to buy aspirin at forty percent off suggested list, a shiny new
    briefcase to hold his assorted junk mail:

he comes here because he can't stand the threatening four
    walls of his room,
he comes here to feel the movement of people, hear the sound
    of a human voice,
he comes here simply to nod off undisturbed, to be left totally
    alone
as he waits very patiently for death to call out his name.

A LETTER TO ARCHIBALD LAMPMAN

Dear Archie:
if I remember correctly
it was in 1888
that you published your first book of verse
Among the Millet
with a legacy left to your wife.

I believe the book was published
or at any rate printed
by J. Durie & Son
of Ottawa, the city you worked in
and died in,
the city that has done exactly nothing
for you its most distinguished citizen
(for my money anyway);

and eighty-six years later
or 1974 to be precise,
you are still too big a risk
to be published in that city.

"A volume this size
concentrated on one poet
would be a risky venture."

Now, I don't blame my publisher
who happens to locate in Ottawa,
and I can't fault your verse—
let's face it, it's the best we have,
you are not in any sense "minor"—

I can only blame it, Archie,
on your misfortune to be born
a poet in a country

so rich and so big
yet so minor as Canada.

FOUND POEM: LOUIS RIEL ADDRESSES THE JURY

Your Honours, Gentlemen of the Jury:
it would be easy for me today to play insanity,
because the circumstances are such as to excite any man
and under the natural excitement of what is taking place today
(I cannot speak English very well,
but I am trying to do so
because most of those here speak English),
under the excitement which my trial causes me
would justify me not to appear as usual,
but with my mind out of its ordinary condition.
I hope, with the help of God,
I will maintain calmness and decorum
as suits the Honourable Court, this Honourable Jury....

Your Honours, Gentlemen of the Jury:
if I was a man of today
perhaps it would be presumptuous
to speak in that way,
but the truth is good to say,
and it is said in a proper manner,
and it is not without presumption,
it is not because I have been libelled for fifteen years
that I do not believe myself something.
I know that through the grace of God
I am the founder of Manitoba;

I know that though I have no open road for my influence,
I have big influence concentrated,
as a big amount of vapour
in an engine. I believe
by what I have suffered for fifteen years,
by what I have done for Manitoba
and the people of the North West,
that my words are worth something,
if I give offence I do not speak to insult. . . .

As to religion, what is my belief?
What is my insanity about that?
My insanity, Your Honours, Gentlemen of the Jury,
is that I wish to leave Rome aside
inasmuch as it is the cause of division
between the Catholics and Protestants.
I did not wish to force my views
because, in Batoche, to the half-breeds that followed me,
I used the word *carte blanche*.

If I have any influence in the New World
it is to help in that way,
and even if it takes
two hundred years to become practical,
then after my death that will bring out practical results,
and then my children will shake hands
with the Protestants of the New World
in a friendly manner.
I do not wish these evils
which exist in Europe to be continued
as much as I can influence it, among the half-breeds.
I do not wish that to be repeated in America,
that work is not the work of some days or some years
it is the work of hundreds of years.

79

My condition is helpless,
so helpless that my good lawyers
and they have done it with conviction
(Mr. Fitzpatrick in his beautiful speech
has proved he believed I was insane),
my condition seems to be so helpless
that they have recourse to try and prove insanity,
to try and save me that way.

If I am insane, of course I don't know it,
it is a property of insanity
to be unable to know it.
But what is the kind of mission that I have?
Practical results.
It is said that I had myself acknowledged
as a prophet by the half-breeds.
The half-breeds have some intelligence.
Capt. Young who has been so polite and gentle
during the time I was under his care,
said that what was done at Batoche
from a military point of view was nice,
that the line of defence was nice,
that showed some intelligence.
It is not to be supposed
that the half-breeds acknowledge me as a prophet
if they had not seen
that I could see something into the future.
If I am blessed without measure
I can see something into the future,
we all see into the future more or less.

As to what kind of prophet would I come?
Would it be a prophet who could all the time
have a stick in his hand and threatening,
a prophet of evil?
If the half-breeds have acknowledged me as a prophet,
if on the other side priests come and say that I am polite,
if there are general officers, good men,
come into this box and prove that I am polite,
prove that I am decent in my manners,
in combining all together you have a decent prophet...

I am glad that the Crown has proved
that I am the leader of the half-breeds
in the North West. I will perhaps be one day acknowledged
as more than a leader of the half-breeds,
and if I am will have an opportunity
of being acknowledged as a leader of good
in this great country....

... If it is any satisfaction to the doctor to know
what kind of insanity I have,
if they are going to call my pretentions insanity,
I say, humbly, through the grace of God
I believe I am the prophet of the New World....
The only things I would like to call your attention to
before you retire to deliberate, are:
1st. That the House of Commons, Senate,
and ministers of the Dominion who make laws for this land
and govern it are no representation whatever
of the people of the North West.

2ndly. That the North West Council
generated by the Federal government
has the great defect of its parent.
3rdly. The number of members
elected for the Council by the people
make it only a sham representative legislature
and no representative Government at all.

British civilization, which rules today the world,
and the British constitution has defined such Government
as this is which rules the North West Territory
as irresponsible Government,
which plainly means that there is no responsibility,
and by the science which has been shown here yesterday
you are compelled to admit it,
there is no responsibility, it is insane.

Good sense combined with scientific theories
lead to the same conclusion.

By the testimony laid before you during my trial,
witnesses on both sides made it certain that petition after
        petition
has been sent to the Federal Government,
and so irresponsible is that Government to the North West,
that in the course of several years besides doing nothing
to satisfy the people of this great land,
it has hardly been able to answer once
or to give a single response.
That fact would indicate lack of responsibility
and therefore insanity complicated with paralysis.

The ministers of an insane and irresponsible Government
and its offspring the North West Council
made up their mind to answer my petitions
by surrounding me slyly and by attempting
to jump upon me suddenly and upon my people
in the Saskatchewan. Happily, when they appeared
and showed their teeth to devour, I was ready;
that is what is called my crime of high treason
and for which they hold me today.
Oh, my good Jurors, in the name of Jesus Christ
the only one who can save and help me,
they have tried to tear me to pieces.

If you take the plea of the defence,
that I am not responsible for my acts,
acquit me completely, since I have been quarrelling
with an insane and irresponsible Government.
If you pronounce in favour of the Crown,
which contends that I am responsible,
acquit me all the same.
You are perfectly justified in declaring
that having my reason and sound mind
I have acted reasonably and in self-defence,
while the Government, my accuser,
being irresponsible and consequently insane,
cannot but have acted wrong,
and if high treason there is,
it must be on its side
and not on my part,

your Honours, Gentlemen of the Jury.

SECOND DIV

"Outside Verrières
a snub-nosed Panther
had our company pinned down
spitting instant death,
so I didn't even have to be smart
to know what was coming next,
and the first chance I got
buggered off to an orchard,
lay there sweating it out."

"Sure enough our two-pip wonder
calls for a PIAT gunner
to lay a couple at the Panther,
and asks of course for me
because he hates my guts the most."

"But before they can look for me
my pal Dickie Driscoll,
the platoon comedian,
tells the lieutenant
without cracking a smile:
'Mac went for a shit
and the wolves must of got him,'
which two-pip doesn't find
the least bit funny,
and mad as hell orders Dickie
to shoulder the PIAT
instead of yours truly."

"So Driscoll of course
who's a lucky bastard,
crawls out and makes
a fantastic hit
with his first grenade,
then his luck runs out
as he starts to crawl back—
an SS bullet
drills a hole through his head."

"All of which you could say
makes me a coward;
so you call it cowardice,
I call it keeping alive. . . ."

THE GIRLS OF THE CRAZY HORSE SALOON

The girls of the Crazy Horse Saloon
have the sharpest, firmest breasts in all the world,
but, alas, they may be fondled only by the eye,
they're set to go pop, pop, pop at the jab of midnight. . . .

The girls of the Crazy Horse Saloon
have the plumpest, roundest backsides in all the world,
but, alas, they may be pinched only by the eye,
they're set to shake to little bits at the throb of midnight. . . .

The girls of the Crazy Horse Saloon
have the longest, slenderest legs in all the world,
but, alas, they may be stroked only by the eye,
they're set to snap in two at the crack of midnight. . . .

The girls of the Crazy Horse Saloon
have the softest, moistest lips in all the world,
but, alas, they may be forced only by the eye,
they're set to zip up tight at the plunge of midnight. . . .

PICTURES OF A LONG-LOST WORLD

Antoine de Saint-Exupéry, July 31, 1944, Poretta, Italy

You can imagine if you wish as he drives from his billet to the base through the now-awakened Tuscany morning that he remembers his first heart-fluttering flight, gift of that boyhood holiday of 1912, with Jules Védrines of the handlebar moustache taking him soaring above the fields of Saint-Maurice-de-Rémens, skimming poplars and cattle-barns, waking the budding poet to an outburst of verses.

Or instead imagine as he's squeezed into the special flying suit, the bulging overalls (his left arm's partly paralyzed), that he suddenly remembers his first flight for Latécoère—the Mont-audran–Casablanca run—studying his map of Spain so hard the night before, ending up having little sleep (like today) and being bumped along on an early-morning bus to that other airfield; then, ready for all kinds of terrors, to fly down without any trouble; but on the way back a far different story—caught by fog and mist forced to crash-land near the airport, and telling his rescuer: "The plane is intact. I apologize for not having completed my first mail flight: I did my best." Such were those early mail-carrying days!

And further imagine as his unarmed Lightning fighter clears the Poretta airstrip, headed for another mapping mission, this one to Grenoble, east of Lyon (but still very much enemy territory, with sleek, death-dealing Messerschmitts, Focker-Wulfs always ready to cobra-strike the untried, the unwary), that he's reliving those Aéropostale days—days of 1930 in lonely Argentina—and perhaps that one week of anguish and exhaustion in mid-July flying a Laté 26 with open cockpit day in day out down the Western Andes slopes, searching for Guillaumet missing on a flight from Santiago, dipping into hidden valleys, banking off from overhanging cliffs always high above him, staggering out half-frozen at the flight's end, but never quite giving up, always full of hope, then the seventh day—rescue!—Guillaumet on his own walking out of the mountains more or less alive. . . .

And then as his Lightning finds its vapour-trail ceiling, fades away in the sun-filled morning, heading out toward his beloved, ravaged France, could he not be thinking of Orly, May of 1940, when slightly earlier that morning he'd taken off in his Bloch 174 to low-fly over Arras on reconnaissance, the fighter escort leaving him just before the doomed city showed, glowing like an iron on an anvil in the midst of green landscape, the ack-ack searching them out at 600 feet, the earth below blazing with rising, golden sparks of the tracers, the bursting shells rocking and shaking the aircraft, then with a shudder one shell exploding right below them, bursting an oil tank and sending the oil gauge flickering wildly to his gaze— and that was the end of that mission, with only good luck getting their punctured sieve back to Orly.

And, as we have said, one can imagine all, some or none of it —the man himself never landed again to tell one word of this, his sixteenth sortie—PILOT DID NOT RETURN AND IS PRESUMED DEAD—that lumbering, bald-on top giant disappearing without leaving a trace, without a last cry for help or of farewell, that turbulent man we've grown to love keeping right to the end the secret of his last most intriguing mystery, lost in the limitless reaches of the sky he charted out as no man then or since, ending somewhere between wind, sand and stars—as would have been the last dying wish of Saint-Exupéry, pilot.

PICTURES OF A LONG-LOST WORLD

*Funeral oration by Anatole France at the Grave of Emile Zola,
Paris, 1902*

A found poem for John Robert Colombo

"Having to recall the struggle
upon which Zola entered in the cause of truth and justice,
is it possible for me to preserve silence
respecting those who were bent on ruining
the cause of an innocent man,
those who felt that if he should be saved,
they would be lost,
and who with all the desperate audacity of fear
therefore strove to overwhelm him?
How can I remove them from your gaze,
when I have to show you Zola
rising, weak and unarmed, before them?
Can I remain silent about their lies?
That would mean silence
as to his heroic rectitude.
Can I remain silent about their crimes?
That would mean silence
as to his virtues.
Can I remain silent about the outrages and slanders
with which they pursued him?
That would mean silence
as to his reward and honours.
Can I remain silent about their shame?
That would mean silence
as to his glory.
No! I will speak out.

With the calmness and firmness
which the spectacle of death imparts,
I will recall the dim days
when egotism and fear had their seats
in the government councils.
People were beginning to know something of the iniquity,
but it was supported, defended
by such public and secret powers
that the most resolute hesitated.
Those whose duty it was to speak out,
remained silent. Some of the best,
who feared nothing personally,
dreaded lest they should involve their party
in frightful dangers. Led astray by monstrous lies,
excited by odious declamation,
the multitude of the people, believing they were betrayed,
grew exasperated. . . . The darkness thickened. Sinister silence
    reigned.
And it was then that Zola addressed
to the President of the Republic
that well-measured, yet terrible letter
which denounced falsity and collusion.

With what fury was he assailed by the criminals,
by their interested defenders, by their involuntary accomplices,
by coalitions of all the reactionary parties,
by the deceived multitude. You saw innocently-minded people
joining in all simplicity
the hideous cortège of hireling brawlers.
You heard the howls of rage and the cries of death
which pursued him even into the *Palais de Justice*
during that long trial when he was judged in voluntary
    ignorance,
or false testimony, amid the clatter of swords.

I see here some of those who then stood beside him,
who shared his dangers.
                    Let them say too
with what firmness he endured it!
Let them say if his robust kindness, his manly pity,
ever deserted him, if his constancy
was for a moment shaken!

In those abominable days
more than one good citizen despaired
of the salvation of the country,
of the moral fortune of France. . . .
But all was saved. Not only had Zola
revealed a judicial error, he had denounced the conspiracy
of all the forces of violence and oppression
leagued together to slay social justice,
Republicanism, freedom of thought in France.
His courageous words awoke the country. . . .

And Zola deserved well of the country
by refusing to despair of justice in France.
We must not pity him for having endured and suffered.
Let us rather envy him!
                    Set above the most prodigious heap
of outrages ever raised by folly, ignorance, malice,
his glory attains to inaccessible heights.
Let us envy him: he honoured his country and the world
by immense literary work, by a great deed.
Let us envy him: his destiny and his heart
gave him the grandest fate: in him at one moment
was set the conscience of mankind!"

THE PRISONER

For Randy

If you can be kept
behind bars long enough,
if you can be made
to endure enough hurt,

then perhaps you'll atone
for my crimes
my uncounted sins
as well as your own.

RACCOON

In the feeble glare of my flashlight
he leisurely climbs
seven rungs of the TV tower
to the bungalow roof, where he crouches
along the eavestrough, waits my next move
with the dull orange floodlights of his eyes
burning through the darkness at me.

I stand there in the three AM night
with nothing more really on my mind
than the silly thought of whether his moustaches
would carry the smell of grapefruit rinds,
assorted greases, rotting bread, tea-leaves,
all that beautiful mixed-together swill
lying in the tipped-over garbage can
on my neighbour's driveway. But I'll never know,
there's no way I'll get any nearer
to my animal than I am right now,
and it's cold standing here in the yard,

so with a last look taking in
the long, striped tail, brown underbelly,
the delicately thin ferret head
and above all that orange-electric stare,

I go inside, shut my window so I won't
hear the sound of that garbage can again
being rocked back and forth, re-enter bed,

while no doubt my animal returns
to the rest of his dinner, slightly annoyed
at this unreasonable interruption,

while my annoyance quickly dies
at being awakened from a deep-down sleep,
already looking forward to our next
strange, but so predictable encounter.

SPRING

Rain beats down
roots stretch up.

They'll meet
in a flower.

GROWTH RATE

When the weeds
on his grass grow long
the old man his neighbour tells him,
"They're growing faster
than Jewish interest."

My Ulster grandmother
could have told them both:
hate and intolerance
grow even faster.

LOMBARD STREET, ONE PM

Not dead drunk
or he wouldn't be writhing like that
half up half down

(his faithful, empty bottle
of old snakeye lying beside him).

Right now the heat
of six blowtorches attacks his stomach wall,
so he's not thinking much about his strategic location
twenty feet from the coroner's office
with ten swift ambulances standing by in the garage,

but it's possible they could have him
in the emergency at St. Michael's
in two minutes flat

and of course have him back
on a coroner's slab
in almost the same time,

so all that has to happen now
is for him to get lucky for once
and be allowed to die.

1975

The present's all confusion,
the future hangs over us
sickeningly ominous,

while the past tempts
with the wisdom of losers
the hindsights of the grave.

KNIFE-SHARPENER

The bell of the knife-sharpener
going by down the street

more solemn than church bells
more plaintive than a bell-buoy
on troubled water

more tired than the feet
of the old man dragging his cart
more weary than the arm
needed less with each passing day.

JOHN A.

How can you be angry for long
at a man who's hoisted up on a platform
half-drunk at election-time,
feels sick but holds it back
until he's asked to address the meeting,
then starts off with these words:
"Here's what I think of the policies
of my honourable opponent"
and timing it beautifully
throws up on the platform,
while the audience goes wild?

Or who wires D'Arcy McGee
at his home in Quebec City:
THERE'S ONLY ROOM
FOR ONE DRUNK IN THE CABINET,
MYSELF.
                    YOURS TRULY, JOHN A.

STRANGE CHANCE

Whatever the strange chance
that threw these two together—

single morning-glory
pushing up out of the clay
of the monster flower urn,

empty Coke can
sun glinting off
its candy-cane sides—

seems to cry out this age.

TIME TO GO

I imagine Death tiptoeing in
one of these heat-crazed evenings
to your hospital bedroom,

and taking you by the hand
saying only: "Come, child, it's time to change
into one of your white confirmation dresses
before your mother finds you here,"

and you without any hesitation follow,
casting one long last look behind
at your tired-out, life-weary body
left there on the bed,

tiptoeing out
like the obedient, trusting child you always were.

IN FLIGHT

Bird that I never thought
would fly again—

when I uncupped my hand
and lifted you toward the eaves,
expecting at the most
the weakest wing-flutter;

instead of which you soared up
and were gone, frail flash—

my whole being
for one glorious moment
winged with you.

"THE LORD HELPS THOSE"

"The Lord helps those
who help themselves"

but so many nice people
have helped themselves to so much

that any Lord who helps them now
is no Lord of mine.

AUGUST

Cicada
high in the tree's shade—a
buzz-saw with bee's
drone, soft sibilance of seas!

ON THEIR WAY TO THE PLAYGROUND

On their way to the playground
four-year-old dark-haired boy
holding hands so lovingly, naturally,
with four-year-old blond-haired girl.

Fifteen years from today
will they still want to,
still be able
to hold hands the same—

dark-haired Negro boy,
white girl with the same golden hair?

FROM AN OLD ADMIRER

Seen from my back window
4.30 of an August morning,
your cold white light tracing its shadow
across the lawn still somehow cheers me
still somehow warms me.

I don't really care
how many heroes of outer space
have landed on you,
scuffed around your dust,
then flew off back to earth
in their infernal flying machines:

for me at least
you've lost none of your mystery
cool riding goddess,

you're still regally imperial
unknowable
unreadable

to this earth man
still somehow divine.

THE FERRY

I was late starting out for the waterfront,
and when I reached the docks
my ferry was already waiting.

A face up there in the wheelhouse looked familiar
so I cried out: "Saul, what's a nice-looking Jewish boy like you
doing in a set-up like this?"

He smiled as he answered me:
"They've got a great five-pin bowling league
over on the Other Side, it's good clean work,
and besides I was getting damn tired
driving streetcars for the TTC.
                         (Incidentally,
they've changed 'Saul' to 'Charon,'
how does that grab you, old round-house curver?)
Now hop aboard, we've got to get this tub moving—
I'll get even worse than Hell
if we're too late crossing over. . ."

EIGHT PEARS

Placed there
in the big picture-window
to catch the morning
and afternoon sun,

eight yellow-green
slightly rotund &
very solemn pears

continue to be stubborn
stay hard

fearing our greedy
two sets of teeth
eager to pierce their skins
dig deep into heavenly juices.

Eight pears
sit there in that window

hating the sun
& fighting time
that ripens everything.

THE GIST OF IT

For Cid

Once we both thought we'd save the world
with poetry.
              Now we're still waiting
to see if we've even saved ourselves.

MULBERRY

In this October
April is pressed back
in your every leaf.

ONE-QUARTER PEOPLE

One-quarter of the world
will die from too many calories,
three-quarters from too few.

One-Quarter People,
the fat roll around our bellies
sags with the weight
of countless corpses
born and yet unborn.

MAUTHAUSEN

"One of the forms of punishing prisoners in Auschwitz was to send them to the quarries of Mauthausen."

One
hundred
eighty
six
steps

count
them

stone steps smoothly laid
each twice as wide
as a man lying beaten
as a man lying pick-axed
as a man lying skull-crushed

one who can no longer
carry rocks at a run
or has annoyed the guards
or has stopped for a moment
or has weakened from hunger

one not allowed
the luxury of leaping
from the cliffs above,
of being crushed
under piles of rock

or shot at the wall
or drowned in the pit
or burnt in the ovens.

"Vienna is horrified,"
the *Sunday Times*
11 January, 1942.

Still, the work goes on,
corpses pile up
on trucks, furnaces
glow blood-red, night-long,

shaking legs
lift stones
their own death
to their backs

    up
    up
    up

in snow
ice
rain

toward hell
not heaven

toward darkness
not light

one
hundred
eighty
six
steps

count
them

"On the north bank
of the Danube,
nestling in lush
hilly countryside
fourteen miles
from Linz"

remember them

never while you draw breath
forget them

keep counting them
forever.

PICTURES FROM A LONG-LOST WORLD

July 20, 1944, Germany: "Stauffenberg's Day"

The night before in his dream
he's again nineteen, just before
he'd entered the Army. The scene is Switzerland,
Minusio, his brothers and twelve friends
are mounting a vigil for twenty-four hours
around the death-bed of his friend, his poet,
Stefan George. . .
                    then suddenly he's awake
in the early dawn, a young Army colonel
in a small room in Berlin, for whom this day
could be the biggest in his life. . . .

While he shaves and dresses
in his brother's apartment, he thinks back five days
to July fifteenth, when he'd flown to the *Wolfsschanze*
far in East Prussia, where he'd hoped to blow Der Führer,
Himmler, Goering, to little pieces. But Hitler's closest pals
hadn't shown up, and cool as an iceberg
he'd given himself the order: Claus, hold off
(although the *Valkyrie* plan had gone ahead
on schedule back there in Berlin,
and he and the rest of the conspirators
very lucky to go undiscovered. . .).

So today, no more compromise:
he'll make another try at the Wolf's Lair,
and this time all he wants is Hitler,
they'll worry about the others later. . .

Any doubts he may have had the night before
when he'd prayed in the Dahlem church
have completely vanished now. He remembers
Bonhöffer's words, a Christian's response
to the age-old question: "How can you reconcile
your part in murder with your faith in God,
with the Ten Commandments?" and his answer:
"If I, as a pastor, see a drunken driver
racing at high speed down the Kurfurstendamm,
it's not only my duty
to bury the victims, comfort the relatives,
but also to wrench the wheel
from the hands of the drunkard."

Now Dietrich's in prison,
his lips sealed about the conspiracy, waiting, waiting
like them all for the death of the Madman. . . .

Calmly he says goodbye
to his brother Berthold, who wishes him the best of luck,
is driven to the airfield at Rangsdorf on a day
very warm, oppressive, an omen of things to come,
he thinks. Shortly afterward takes off
in an old noisy Heinkel
for the ride to Rastenburg, with "Poison Dwarf" General
    Stieff,
a tiny, hunchbacked conspirator, passing over
two small parcels to be carefully placed in his briefcase,
each containing one two-pound bomb. The second bomb's
for insurance, just in case the first one fails
for any reason, which they pray it will not. . . .

Almost too soon he's landing at Rastenburg, and the nine-
    mile drive
to the *Wolfsschanze* begins. Now the die's cast
he wonders how his friends, his fellow conspirators
are doing—von Stulpnagel in Paris, Beck, von Treschow,
General Olbricht, von Witzleben, in Berlin—
no doubt by now they're already pacing floors,
smoking too many cigarettes, waiting
for Fellgiebel's message, the magic word "Valkyrie"....

But he forces his thoughts back to the car
in which they're riding, thoughts almost as sombre
as the dark gloomy forest they're entering now;
on, past the outer, then inner check-points
of the Lair, where he and his adjutant Häften
head for the officers' mess
and a late breakfast with the Commandant's aide.

Before long it's noon, time to join
Field-Marshal Keitel: he finds himself with the fussy Chief of
    Staff,
who tells him the meeting's half an hour sooner.
So, only twenty minutes left, with the bomb still
to be activated!
                    Very cooly he finds himself asking
Keitel's ADC if there's somewhere he can go
to wash, then change his shirt. And imagine the scene
in the ADC's quarters as he and Häften unwrap
one of the bombs (Häften doing
most of the unwrapping, as Stauffenberg
has no right hand or forearm and only two fingers
and a thumb on his left: barely able in fact
to start the bomb's mechanism, and that only after
the most careful practice. . .)

114

which he manages now, thank God,
and they stuff the bomb into his briefcase
along with his papers and shirts, hurry out to join Keitel
who's chafing at the delay, then grouses even more
when he finds the meeting already started
on reaching the conference room (which is just as well,
as the bomb in that briefcase is timed to go off
in ten to fifteen minutes from now. . . .)
                           There's Hitler bent over
one of the war maps, hearing more bad news
from the Eastern Front made as palatable as possible.
Neither Himmler nor Goering are present,
which doesn't worry him now. What does worry him
is the conference room itself, made of wood lightly reinforced
with concrete. Not nearly as good for his purpose
as the usual bunker, and with these wide-open windows
because of the heat, the blast will be greatly diminished. . . .

But once he moves over to the table,
slips his briefcase first to the floor,
then pushes it farther under the table
almost at Hitler's feet, he feels better, breathes easier,
Hitler will not escape today!

So anxious to leave before he can be asked for his report,
he makes an excuse about a telephone call from Berlin,
and before anyone can stop him,
walks quickly out of the room, down the hall,
and right outside into the humid air,
crosses over to the check-point of the innermost control,
strides through it taking a salute and across the compound
where von Häften's waiting with the staff car along with
    Fellgriebel

who'll flash the signal back to Berlin
after the explosion, thus begin the revolt.

Just as he reaches the car with its engine running,
the explosion comes (12.42 by his watch), a deafening sound
telling him of certain sweet success;
and without a pause they race off
to pass through the other two check-points,
(the first without any trouble, the second more nerve-racking,
and requiring a call to the Duty Officer
when the guards refuse to let him pass)....
                              Then, on the open road,
speeding for their waiting aircraft, he throws out
the pieces of the second bomb as they race along,
each piece of it symbolic, last fragments
of the Hitler yoke now being tossed aside....

Lastly, their plane takes off for Berlin, and all the long
three hours back his heart sings, his life has reached its highest
    meaning.
He believes that God somehow spared him in Africa
to accomplish this task. Now, nothing can stop them,
not all the timid souls left in Berlin
(he'll make sure of that!), with Germany
saved at the eleventh hour, his beloved fatherland
saved for his children and his childrens' children....

Success, success, success, the whirling propeller
of their tired old Heinkel seems to roar back to him....

RAID ON THE RUHR

For Art Servage

Bomb selection switches on,
arming switch, bombsight switch okay,
repeater compass in good working order,
altimeter shipshape—

this, his last check made ahead of time,
left him a minute when he leaned back on his knees
in the bombardier's compartment and looked out
ahead through the moulded perspex nose
of "O" for "Oboe" at the darkness streaked
with yellow beams of searchlights, red, green-blue
of sky-markers, brown puffs of flak-fire,
and dead ahead the ghost-black silhouette
of a Hally banking hard into its bomb-run....

Then he'd had his eyeful of hell: tried to forget
his heart beating faster, sweat underneath his armpits,
frozen feet, cold hands, their four engines' body-shaking roar,
tried to bring all his mind's focus back to the head
of his bombsight in front of him swaying
a little like a cobra to the aircraft's motion,

with him the snake-charmer soon to be called
to do his little trick with the bombsight's hairlines,
dropping his twelve canisters one per second
into the growing crimson glow, sending his cargo
of incendiaries whistling down: stoking the fire-storms,
blackening the ruins, piling high the corpses,
("we're going to shift the rubble around a little"
was the way the Briefing Officer had put it)....

He crouched now, eyes only on his pet snake,
counting the minutes
to death or deliverance.

OCTOBER LEAVES

What if this afternoon
all good citizens like me
sallied forth with rakes
firm in hand, attacked our leaves
with relentless fury, piling up
the crinkled harvest until streets,
cars, trees, even houses disappeared
under the flood, and we ourselves
caught in the rustling jungles
of our own making,
cried out, "enough"
one choking avalanche too late?

SPIRIT OF 1775–1975

General Richard Montgomery, American commander:
"I'll have my Christmas dinner in Quebec
or die in the attempt."
                              So died in the attempt,
along with many of his men, the strips of paper
reading "Liberty or Death" they carried in their caps,
buried with their corpses in the snows of Lower Town.

1775, year of the first invasion
of Canada by the Americans. Losers at first,
they never quite gave up trying; even General Brock
couldn't stem the tide forever.

Now by 1975
they've completely conquered us.
Not with arms
but with dollars, not with love
but by sharp Yankee trading.

General Richard Montgomery didn't get his Christmas dinner
in Quebec City.
                    Instead, a few years later,
Benjamin Franklin got the 49th Parallel
and the Ohio Valley, which he reckoned
was worth a defeat or two, many Christmas dinners. . . .

WATCHING THE GOOD NOISE SLOWLY DIE

In the TV short we are watching
an older Dickie Wells walks down Wall Street
with a briefcase full of securities,
(he's a messenger for a New York broker)—

then it's cut to a private jam session
where Dickie coaxes great riding sound
out of his slick-sliding trombone—

and on to a shot of Jo Jones
as he opens a street-door, climbs the stairs
to a second-storey music store in Harlem
where he sells drums, gives drumming lessons—

moving back to the session again
where he makes his talking drum
the pulsing background for a riff played the old
Count Basie way—
                    shift again to hard reality
with Buck Clayton holding forth in the office
of the Musicians' Union where he does paper work
behind a desk—
                    only this time when we switch over
to the jamming it's Joe Newman, not old Buck
lighting the horn's fire (Buck's not playing now
because of health reasons), and fitting too
as Joe took over Clayton's trumpet chair
in the Basie band when the master went to war—

Now a scene with Joe giving a lecture
on his instrument to a group of young Negroes
much the same way he does around the country,
and it's no-nonsense stuff with Joe,
he'll die with that horn held in his hand.

Then a final cut to smiling Earle Warren
as he walks into the dance-hall where he plays
rhumbas, polkas, waltzes, everything but jazz,
but still carrying his head high, giving out
that solid, honest tone—
                                    as he does in the studio,
driving his alto the same way it steamed up
many a bandstand in the reckless, good old years—

with the cameras catching for the last time
the dream-like, contented look
on his and those other sweaty faces
crowded into this rehearsal hall tonight. . . .

And you ask yourself—already knowing the answer—
why does good noise like this ever have to die?

RILKE, DYING

Rilke, dying,
refused all medication to know
the agony of the plunge
to the deepest well-bottom of pain.

Died, they say, with a radiance
shining through his eyes.

THE WHOLE STUPID GAME

Years ago when I met this friend of mine
on the street and he said to me,
"I don't give a damn now for my poems
and the whole stupid game of poetry,
I've still got my books and records,
the rest of it can all go to hell,"

I was so surprised that I hardly answered him,
then the next day felt a little sad
for this good man who felt himself cheated
by the one passion in his life,
because I couldn't understand him at all,
thought his bitterness had turned him slightly mad.

Today, though, I understand him very well,
don't think him the slightest bit mad,
in fact, have often echoed his words,
"Don't give a damn now for my poems
and the whole stupid game of poetry."

VIOLETS, WILD

Just as I had suspected,
once I moved aside
the last layer of dead leaves
with my rake
                lying there
tiny yet enormous with colour,
shivering still but warmly shining,

violets, one or two clumps
of them, in all their defiance
making a liar one more time
of death and all
his winter-bound corpses.

BLOSSOMING

In the night
sifted down

flooding the grass
under each maple

with its own fine
yellowgreensoft rain

THE TREE BY THE HOUSE

Out the very ends
of the two upright branches
sawn off only last year,

two new branches sprout bravely
with a showing of leaves,
as if to say: no hard feelings,
you did what you had to do,
now we're doing the same.

But don't think they're not laughing at me,
those little green bastards!

BIRD WITH A BERRY

A bird with a berry
big as its head tries
to carry it across
the back grass, gets halfway
then drops it.
         When I ask him
why he doesn't pick it up again
he answers, "I'm just not
in the mood and besides
I'd probably only choke
on the damn thing anyway,"

which only proves birds
are no better than humans
at answering questions.

THE BRIDGE

You may not believe it
but this morning I noticed
a gorge-spanning bridge
of spider-rope drawn
between two long volumes
on my bookcase's top.

And in case you're still interested
those two titles were:
The Voice by Robert Desnos,
(and again I repeat
you may not believe it—)

The Spider Hangs Too Far from the Ground
by Antonio Cisneros!

PICTURES OF A LONG-LOST WORLD

Duty Storekeeper, RCAF

It's late summer, 1942. We are losing the War
but no-one thinks to tell us. Even the act
of carrying rifles around camp
makes little sense when we have no bullets
(they're all safely locked up somewhere).

But tonight I'm Duty Storekeeper,
which means 5 PM to 8 AM
I'm at anybody's call
who wants things in a hurry.
                              Things like gasoline,
100 octane, three tender-loads, the last
at 3 AM, a simple transaction
ending up like something out of a movie,
and a bad one at that—me driving over
to the gas dump with the MT driver,
and no sooner down at the bowzer
than a big security guard appears out of nowhere,
half-staggering on his feet, slurring his words,
points his rifle at us and says he'll shoot
if we take one more step—
                              I know the clown well,
a hard-drinking, hard-headed Nova Scotian,
so take him at his word,
and for a small eternity
the two of us sweat it out trying
to talk some sense into him—

                              which we finally do,
and I'm glad, he's a nice guy really,
only booze has turned him crazy-mad tonight—
and we get the gas finally, wave goodbye to our guard,
and I come back here to the Equipment Section
to unwind a little, still slightly shaken,
so that it takes me an hour or two
to get the thought out of my mind of that gas dump going up
in one flaming sea of fire, all two hundred thousand gallons,
if a rifle bullet had somehow struck
in the wrong place. . . .
                              I try to sleep finally
in the bed in the Orderly Room, and for a while
the bedlam of half a dozen engines revving up
in Number One Hangar right across the road
keeps me wide awake. But finally their constant roar
of thunder nods me off, and I dream
my favourite dream of taking off at dawn
down the runway in a Hudson,
circling our station once, then heading out to blue water,
where, hugging the coast running south we leave Cape Breton,
and before long the sand dunes of Sable Island
stretch out below us: we swoop down, the boys open fire with
      their .45s
on a herd of wild ponies (aiming high over their heads),
and they gallop like the wind away from us, their small shapes
      struggling
through the sand plains: and for a moment I'm an animal
      myself
like those below, free, like the wind, to come and go,
no war in my heart, no enemy to seek out and kill,
only the clear sky above, the uncomplicated blue all around
      me,
every trouble, every worry blown suddenly away
with no trace left in the shifting, dazzling sand. . . .

AWAITING THE FIRST DROP

No-one knows
the exact moment
of what hour
the first drop of rain will fall

but after one whole week
of blinding sun
of scorched grass
of wilting leaves

it somehow seems important

so I watch and wait
along with the birds
along with the ants
along with every living
breathing thing

that first heavy
cool splash of a raindrop
to wet the page
of this poem about the rain.

NIGHT OUT

After the first drink
lightens the front of your head,
the faces of the city
light up for no reason,
become more alive, more human,
and the words you hear them speak
more forceful, more at ease,
than you imagined possible
from these programmed lives,
these computerized brains,
these data-banked responses.

After the second drink
lightens the back of your head,
these buildings which block out the sun
(and store in their giant hives
piled-up honeycombs of slave-bees,
released at five, recalled at nine)
take on a majesty
of soaring glass and metal
the eye blinks at now
in wondering disbelief.

After the third drink
sets the stomach glowing,
you can remember men
once hated hard enough to kill,
and suddenly they seem
weak, more to be pitied
for their vices, their stupidity,
even worthy of forgiveness;

you decide that the simple act
of bringing them to life again
gives them an importance
never once deserved.

After the fourth drink
tingles in your left toe,
you see so clearly
as if for the first time,
how all your grand thoughts,
your books, your projects,
are all echoes, re-echoes,
of something done, said before;
how small they seem now
beside living, beside dying,
one more widely-thrown pebble
tossed into the ocean's roar!

After the fifth drink
tingles in your right toe,
you feel there is still time
to start from the beginning,
that nothing is final
or impossible,
nothing finally bad or evil,
unless we allow
the smallness, the poverty
we bring to our lives,
to overwhelm us.

After the sixth drink. . .

WHOSE COLOUR YELLOW IS

Today I learned
whose colour yellow is:

picking up what I thought
a dead robin in the garden,
I turned the bird over
expecting the usual,

and instead was dazzled
by a yellow-downed breast
a yellow-downed belly,
warmth of them glowing
though the body was cold,
warmth of them charging
up my arm
through my shoulder.

Today I learned
yellow is death's colour,

pulsing, throbbing colour!

LITTLE BUSH

I should pull out this stubborn little bush
growing out half between the brick
of the house and the driveway's cement.

This useless little bush
that I haven't the heart
or the hand to uproot,

seeing here a fellow sufferer
even more stubborn
amid all this barrenness
than myself.

THE TRILLIUM RETURNS

Imagine her in the Sixties
moored in some Island lagoon,
slowly rotting through the summer,
aching, shivering through the winter,
her paddle-wheels broken, sides peeled of paint,
boiler rusting, only the cries
of birds, the padding of rodents
to remind her she still lived, served a humble need.

(My father's fondest thought of her
one hot summer evening
when she had hundreds more
than her usual passengers
coming back from Hanlan's
and a Maple Leafs ball-game,
the year 1913,
and how at the city side
she keeled over badly
and for a long minute
Dad thought he'd get
a free swim in the bay,

and my dearest memory
another summer night
in a much later summer,
when I stood at her railing
coming back from the Point,
and fancied I could make out
City Hall's clock-tower
through the mixed hell-black
and hell-flaming crimson
of Toronto's skyline)....

Now imagine her next year (1976)
tied up at Queen's Quay dockside, nervous
as a new bride to have the gang-plank lowered,
the first holidayers come aboard!
New paddle-wheels, shining new superstructure,
new steam-plant! Imagine her joy
when the warning cast-off whistle sounds,
as she clears the dock, heads out into the bay,
feeling her paddle-wheels churning again,
the pulse-beat of her engines!
                              Fairer than ever
this flower of our city's water-gardens,
reborn again, still kindling the dream!

VIC DICKENSON AT BASIN STREET

Why is it the simple act
of him reaching down
to take a round piece of something
like rough canvas, and fitting it
almost casually over
the gleaming mouth of his trombone,

can make me suddenly
sit up straighter in my chair,
with the almost certain feeling
that the first note to come
from that shining instrument will be
more subtle-softer sounding
more singing sweet,

than the last note from before
still lingering, re-echoing,
through my jazz-happy head?

THE CRUTCH

Just by the way he holds the paper bag
in which his twenty-six-ouncer keeps out of sight,
and by the furtive look he gives
each new passenger on the bus, I'm sure
he has this fear that some night soon he's either
going to drop his bottle smash, or someone's
going to grab it out of his arms
and run off with it—
                          leaving him without his crutch
to hobble with along the endless miles
of another evening.

THE DIFFERENCE

You only look at the colour of his skin.

I look into the colour of his heart.

MINOR TESTAMENT

Solzhenitsyn, as I learn
more and more about the miracle
of your life, its heights,
its utter desolations,

I grow more and more ashamed
of my own life, its pitiful
evasions, pretences, easy courage,

follow even further behind
the brilliance of your shadow.

WEATHER

It will either rain
or not rain

the sun either shine
or not shine

wind blow
or not blow.

Thank God at least
for the weather—constancy

is not one of its virtues—
it's tugged, torn and taken

by the unexpected, by the un-
reasonableness of elements

beyond the weatherman's control
or yours or mine—or as some say—

beyond even His.

OF SPARROWS

You never find the corpses
of sparrows the winter claims,
enough wind is around
to send those thin bones,
scrawny feathers far.

You never hear a sparrow
cry out in frozen fear,
make the slightest hunger moan;
they suffer silently,

leaving all the groaning, the fuss,
to you and me
behind the steamy glass,
the walled-in certainty
of our heartless houses.

FIRST DAY OF A NEW YEAR

The year starting well—
good brandy
in my morning coffee,
warm sun bouncing up
from the squeaky snow,
cold air on my cheeks,
and at the top of the climb
a moment to stop
get my breath,
then stride happily ahead.

FIRST ECHO

The day Ernest Hemingway
received his Nobel Prize

I heard the first muffled echo
of that rifle shot ring out.

TO A CONTEMPORARY

It must have been
at least ten years ago
I remember telling you one evening
that poets had no business at all
in universities,
and how for almost half a minute
I was afraid you'd leap
across at me, tear out both my eyes!

Today no-one would deny
your excellence as a poet,
and I'm happy to know
that your Ph. D.
hasn't thrown you into the graveyard
of a university,

where, as the glittering light
of some English Department,
you might have spent your days
dissecting the bones
of long-departed poets,

in your spare time plotting out
piece by piece the details
of your own shining corpse.

AT THE CAKE-AND-DOUGHNUT COUNTER

I was mad at you the other day,
so mad that I stalked away
from your counter without buying anything,
although I was very hungry—and all because
you'd waited on someone else
when it was obviously my turn—
how's that for petty anger?

As usual you had on your face
that same look of mild annoyance
you always seem to have these days,
as if we customers
had no business bothering you
with such petty trifles as being served,
as if you should be left all alone
behind your counter in the five-and-dime
to suffer on without any interruption.

So you're too old to be working,
so your feet hurt
your legs ache,
you can't bend without the greatest effort,
and I suspect your eyes aren't too good
for making proper change,
can't tell a nickel from a quarter,
while even your hands seem to tremble slightly.

But what's all this to do with me?
All I want is my bran muffins
or doughnuts placed in a bag
and handed to me, nothing else,
the rest doesn't really concern me—
take it up with your manager,
write a letter to the Woolworth family.

So the next time I come in, smile,
even say a nice word or two
as you hand me my little bag,
forget how your legs ache,
forget how you can't stand
on your feet a single minute more:

remember I, the customer,
am the one thing that matters in your life,
without me you are nothing,
would be much better off if you were dead.

WAITING FOR BREAK-OUT

All last week I felt restless, ill-at-ease,
with myself and all the world,
and truly couldn't figure out why.

Then this morning walking down
through Langmuir Wood and seeing
only green moss showing on the slopes,
only scattered spears of skunk-cabbage thrusting up,

I knew I still waited with the trees
for three more warm days of sun,
so both of us could break about-to-burst buds,
push out delicate green leaves together!

WAITING FOR THE POEM TO COME THROUGH

For days
for a whole week nothing.

So you sit in the dugout
watching your team-mates
carve out the headlines—
a one-hitter
two home runs back to back—
patiently sweating it out,
waiting for your next chance to come.

When it does,
when you get the nod
from the manager,
in a game
with nothing going right
and a last chance to win—
two out and two on. . .

You feel nervous
yet somehow good
as you step in,
get yourself set
near the back of the box,
take a couple of quick swings
as your mind decides
whether to drive it through the mound
or chop one past first.

Then you're ready,
the umpire behind you
growls "play ball,"
you give that last little wiggle,
look straight ahead at the kid
standing tall on the rubber,
murmur under your breath
"throw it over and duck,"

wait for the poem to come whipping
curving
sinking in.

WAKING UP TO SUMMER

I haven't yet wakened to the day,
my head is still somewhere far away
in the dark, dark places of the night,
I walk with my two feet in rebellion.

Then a perfect stranger
in the back lane says "Beautiful morning"
and half-awake I answer, "Magnificent."

We go our separate ways,
and it's only twenty minutes later
that the sun finally strikes through my eyes, makes me see
why the sky leans over, taps my puzzled head with its finger,
and says, "If you must be blue, be as blue as I am."

Then suddenly I'm wide awake
with the riot of summer
exploding all around me.

And searching for a word
to describe all that's happening,
the echo of a voice half-awake
says "Magnificent,"

only that same voice is awake and singing now. . . .

JUNE ROSES

Your insolent mouths
bending down from branches

(reddest lips of summer
searching out a lover)

kissed only by the sun
tongued only by the wind

turn to me the pouts
of over-spoilt children.

TWIN SEQUENCE

My big cat stepping oh so carefully
in a ten-second sequence
of unimagined grace,
so the bleached strewn petals
of our backyard roses
won't stick to his treads.

And a half-hour later
in a sequence of my own
I can hardly believe happening,

I find myself going through
the same gingerly performance
(but so much less gracefully),

as I cross a stretch of pavement
and am forced to crush under foot
the delicate, scented
once-so-proud chestnut blossoms,

yesterday's white virginal beauties
today's faded invalids in brown.

WHATEVER TURNS YOU ON

Almost over the hill
(which is my age)
he stopped me only yesterday,
and leaning his bald head down,
asked me if I could recommend
a love poem to him—"something
about the early stages"
is how he put it—
which must mean my friend's
head-over-heels in love
with some kid barely twenty
from that sweat shop he works in. . . .

It made me think of what I said
to my wife the first time
she voted for Trudeau:
"It's the weirdest thing
you've ever done in your life,
but whatever turns you on, baby,
whatever turns you on. . ."

TOO SOON FROM THE NEST

Another week in the nest
and your wings could have taken you anywhere,

but this afternoon in the grass
you're a helpless, half-winged
beginning of a bird, and so frightened,
you hardly struggle as I pick you up
in one cupped hand, and mounting a ladder,
place you in a corner of the eaves.

"It'll only die of hunger there,"
my wife says, and she's probably right,
but at least you won't die
after a cat has pawed you for an hour. . . .

Besides, I always allow for miracles,
being a man of hope, and who knows—
God may have time enough to spare
to lift you on His wings,
find another nest for you
in some kinder, saner world.

THE ANNIVERSARY ROSES

For a week the anniversary roses
stained the room more blood-red
than any pin-pricks from our fingers.

Then came their dying.
But you could not, would not
accept that: made a small trench

in a cool corner of the garden,
and planted them with the prayer:
may they live as long as our love.

And not until next summer
will we both know
if we survive or go under.

THE SEASON OF THE SMALL, SMALL SPIDER

It's the season of the small, small spider,
which when it's squashed between the fingers
leaves the slightest green-yellow stain.

A time when leaves die, curl their ends
months ahead of time: when trees die
like that giant horse-chestnut down the street,
which only a week ago had strewn
honeyed blossoms on the walk (as if the effort
of such a lush flowering
had been too much for her
and killed her, earth-mother
taken suddenly in childbirth):

when the grass cries out
from the sheer weight of heat pressed down
layer upon crushing layer: when the songs
of birds become too shrill for joy,
too frenzied for singing's simple pleasure:

when the earth itself chokes
on its own dried-out dust
and spits up only dust—

the season of the small, small spider,
which only the coming of the blessed rain shall end,
O sweet, wild, white, singular falling!

THAT BACK ROOM OF YOURS

I've just been in
that Back Room of yours,
and it's such a tight little
warm little cosy little Place

that I hope you'll soon get rid
of those fat-assed politicians
squatting there like toads
before riding-voting maps
(which they stab to death slowly
with thumbtacks), chain-smoking
their evil cigars and missing
the spittoon two tries in three—

besides, there's really only
enough room for one—
for me!

A SQUIRREL CAN HAVE PROBLEMS TOO

When I first looked out
on our morning garden,
a squirrel was coming
upsidedown a tree,
a green tennis-ball in his mouth.

No, not a tennis-ball
I decided after a second look,
but a rounded tree-fruit;
still, the same kind of problem
for friend squirrel—where to hide it?—
where indeed?

In rapid succession
he tried burying it in the grass,
hiding it in the bushes,
even tried to make it up the tree again,
but none of this satisfied him,
he ran back and forth
looking more ridiculous
with each new hiding-place.

Then suddenly an inspiration—
he approached the house and pushed it. . .

Yes, I'm ending this poem right there,
because where that squirrel finally hid
his problem tree-fruit
is a secret only
the two of us are going to share.

HOSPITAL CORRIDOR

Looking more like eighty
than the sixty-three years
your nurse says you are,

you walk up and down
this hospital corridor
on legs match-stick thin
all day long
then half the night,
because, as you tell the nurse,
"Everyone in my room there hates me."

Which I don't believe,
it's only that they're sick to death
of your endless monologue
that you try on everybody
who comes within earshot:

as I myself
(your latest captive audience)
listened patiently last night
as you told me in detail
of your recent illness,
how you crawled on the floor
from your bed to the bathroom
and back again three days
and three nights
                about your TV stolen
and then your radio,
of your hatred of Toronto,
of your husband dead twenty years,

and how all you want
is to be left alone,
not bothered by anyone
in your tiny apartment,
about your hands being crippled
by arthritis so you can't work
a typewriter any more....

Okay, I had to admit
I couldn't blame you in the least
for hating all the world,
for believing all the people in it
were against you or laughed at you.

But I didn't hate you,
couldn't laugh at you either,
woman·worn out before her time
with the random thoughts of a child,

woman pacing up and down the halls
of this hospital
too big and too busy
to bother about one frail old lady
with a wandering mind,
with only her tongue still able
to lash out at all her real
and imaginary enemies;

some hint of stubborn pride,
her unyielding independence,
all she had left,
unless you count an equally
stubbornly beating heart!

ON THE EDGE

Walking this street going west
into the setting sun I'm locked
so tight in my own thoughts I'm hardly aware
of someone coming toward me:
                              then the glare
of the sun suddenly blinds—I only know
a headless man has passed by,
his coat open like a loose cloak
around him—
                    No, I don't turn around
to see if he's old or young, stranger, whatever,
something tells me not to—
                              and walk on
with the sun slipping over the edge
of my world and me not sure at all
if what passed me was headless
or two-headed, friend or foe:
                              and if this street
this sun—even this world—is real or unreal. . . .

TWO LOST SOULS AT CHRISTMAS TIME

Where Yonge Street meets Queen
the flood of human faces quickens,
seethes in its quicksand run;

and floating on top
face of an Indian boy
either drunk or on drugs
talking softly to people
(the bobbing flotsam passing
circling round)
who try to avoid him.

And at the same moment
on the street's other side
a man striding briskly,
shouting at the top of his voice
in some Slavic language
God only knows what hatred
what bitterness,
that fine deep voice
a slave to inner demons
eating out his soul;

both caught somehow for a moment
along the banks of this flood-stream,
this human tide of Yonge Street,
with only two more shopping days till Christmas
with only two more shopping days of madness,

then suddenly both are swept away
to bob once or twice, then go under...

while down this torrent
sweep fresh faces
cut adrift, swirling helplessly,
at the strange whim and mercy
of this river of the lost and the dead.

A TRICK OF THE MOONLIGHT

A trick of the moonlight
when across the back
of my yard the snow
shows the many-fingered roots
of trees stretching out
in one skeleton x-ray,

which I smugly know
is only the too-naked
branches of my trees
fast frozen in shadow,

then look again out my window,
and am suddenly shattered—
for as hard as I search
there's no trace of moon showing!

THE CRITIC OF POETRY

You are the dog
who, having eaten
his own very fresh vomit,

can't help licking his lips.

AT THREE IN THE MORNING

At three in the morning
someone next door
raising/lowering a blind:

to let in/shut out
the glare of the moonlight?

ONE EX-SANDLOTTER TO ANOTHER

For Elmer Croswell

There's not a good strike left
in our pitching arms, Elmer,
not even the bull-pen coach
of the Expos would give us a second look....

But there were afternoons when our curve ball
bit the outside corner hard, when our fast one
seemed to fly like something on a string
drawn in by the catcher's big mitt,
when the only breeze at Christie Pits
came from the sad bats of the other team
hunting the elusive horsehide
our five fingers tightened on, tossed
plateward.
        Afternoons, Elmer,
that became our own,
that no-one can ever take from us!

BIX STILL LIVES

says the sign above the doorway
of Don's Discs
367A Queen Street East,

but the door's locked
and Don's not around to tell me
where Bix is right now
and how he's making out:

so I can only hope
he's still not playing cornet,
or if he is
that he's forgotten all about jazz,

because if he hasn't
he'll need a lot more
than a flask in his pocket
or a couple of bottles
within reach of his bed

to chase away all the blues
bound to pile up in his head.

THIS DAY

I know he doesn't want it
but this day must contain

not only the sun
the air like springtime

but one man
holding firmly one bottle,
sitting in his own piss
in a liquor-store doorway.

Only then can I feel this sun
breathe deeply this air,

only then can I plan
how I will picture tomorrow.

PICTURES OF A LONG-LOST WORLD

German War Photographer, 1917

The Army photographer
who had the guts
to snap this picture
of a French *poilu*
shot to death in mid-stride
as he almost reaches
the dug-in German gunners
behind which our cameraman
crouches in a shell-hole,

perhaps could have been expected
to feel much more compassion
for this useless slaughter
across the French countryside,

if it wasn't for the fact
that if that *poilu*
or any of his buddies
had made those last ten yards,

he'd be taking himself
a bullet or a bayonet,
and lurching also
suddenly
ridiculously
as he bleeds out his life,

leaving no-one to catch
in a matchless photo
his own colourful departure.

TWO SETS OF FINGERS

Except for my clumsiest beginnings
(which are hardly worth mentioning)

there have always been
two sets of fingers on my pen,

mine and yours,
yours and mine.

Without yours the pen
would not have finished one line

but stopped halfway as if baffled
or fresh out of words.

And yet your name appears nowhere
above, below a single poem.

It is only I know what my debt is
it is only I know your sacrifice.

Let us call these poems if you like
the children we never had,

a thousand-voiced family,
some born hard, some easily,

all bearing, I hope, some marks
of our love, our sweat and our care.

PICTURES FROM A LONG-LOST WORLD

Gas Instruction, Southern England, 1945

With spring winds sweeping from the Channel—
lithe, confident invaders storming warm and fresh across the
    sands
and up the chines past machine-gun posts and wire
    entanglements
into the streets of the town—
                      why are we standing here
with gas-masks in hand, waiting our turn
to enter these low, evil-smelling sheds
as soon as the last group inside staggers out
into the morning sunshine choking at the throat
and eyes running, smarting, with us strangers
forced to laugh at their moment's misery?

Plainly and simply because we are at war,
because even in this year of '45
no-one knows what a desperate enemy will do
when his last V-2 has been used up or captured:

and this is why in a minute or two
we'll go inside, stand looking at each other
through these eye-pieces (creatures born
of some horrible nightmare), then at a command
throw these headpieces off, feel the gas
grip our throats and nostrils, stagger too
out the door in orderly panic, stand in the sun
and blink and cough like those other ones before us;

the sons of men who at Ypres in another war
pissed on their cotton bandoliers, tied them over nose and
    mouth,
and waited for that "greenish, yellow cloud"
of chlorine to come slowly rolling in,
to face death, to die, but to hold the line
against that same enemy we face today....

SOME GRAVESTONE INSCRIPTIONS FOR A CANADIAN PRIME MINISTER WHO DIED YOUNG

1

Made fine babies
few good laws.

2

We dug
his shrug.

3

To hold us together
he forced us apart.

OPERATING ROOM

I'm in an operating room.
The noises it makes
sound very efficient indeed.

Flat on my back
I watch the surgeon slice
pieces of bone from my nose.

I know he is being very careful
for every once in a while
he measures with his calipers
to make sure he cuts in line.

The grating sound of bone snapping,
of bone yielding to his blade,
is the only clue
that what is happening
is almost over,

that soon I'll be wheeled out
of all this efficiency,
back into a world
of easy error,
of casual shrug-of-the-shoulder
carelessness,

along corridors of shining pain,
down bottomless elevators
to rooms hung with deathly shadows.

SOME NOTES ON "THE ROAD-RUNNER"

In Ethiopia
he might have been one
of the Emperor's messengers
delivering letters of state—

but here in Toronto
he's "the Road-Runner"
laughed or smiled at
wherever he goes,
dressed in business suit and tie,
briefcase in his hand,
running-shoes on his feet.

Dark-skinned man of India
perhaps thirty-five years old,
at most one hundred twenty pounds
dripping very wet,

he walks even at a half-trot,
always runs up and down
the steepest escalator.

And now that winter's here
he'll probably move faster
(not wearing an overcoat
because that might slow him down).

Banks and trust companies
know him very well,
though he's seldom in any one office
long enough to say "hello" or "goodbye."

If they'd only let him deliver
all the stocks and bonds on Bay Street
we could close at four every day.

In a city of samenesses
he's even more refreshing
than that first noon-hour beer.

And as for all those
who laugh at him—how many
will ever do anything
beautiful or silly enough
to draw even laughter?

One question though's unanswered—
how many pairs of running-shoes
does he wear out in a year?

(For the past week
since he's switched to Adidas
he seems to have stepped up
the pace even more!)

SUICIDE IN THE SUBWAY

Jumped too eagerly.